Alexz

Not sur
going next but heres a
starting point for your travel
fund.
Love you always-
Christy

Alexz
I Am forever greatful that
you came into our life
you have a beautiful spirit
and I pray that it always
shines
Love you

chuck

THE ULTIMATE

travel

PLANNER + JOURNAL

crafted
travel company

Published by Crafted Travel Company
2 Via Silla
Rancho Santa Margarita, CA 92688
www.craftedtravelco.com

ISBN: 978-1-7373535-0-8

"We travel not to escape life, but for life not to escape us."

- ANONYMOUS

crafted travel
C
company

Created by travel professionals to help you plan and organize your upcoming vacation. We didn't stop there, however. We've also included journal and memory pages so you can write and keep momentos from your vacation. In the end you'll have a beautiful permanent keepsake of your journey.

If you need assistance at any point in planning your vacation, please feel free to contact us at hello@craftedtravelco.com or www.craftedtravelco.com. We would be happy to help in any way!

Bon Voyage!

Crafted Travel Company

TABLE OF CONTENTS

Passenger + Emergency Information

passenger information

EMERGENCY CONTACT AT HOME:

TRAVEL INSURANCE/TRAVEL EMERGENCY PHONE + POLICY NUMBER:

PASSENGER 1 (FULL NAME AS SPELLED ON PASSPORT OR ID)

PASSPORT NUMBER, EXPIRATION, + ISSUE DATE:

TSA PRECHECK OR GLOBAL ENTRY NUMBER:

AIRLINE MEMBERSHIP NUMBER:

NOTES (HEALTH/MEDICAL ALERT/PREFERENCES)

PASSENGER 2 (FULL NAME AS SPELLED ON PASSPORT OR ID)

PASSPORT NUMBER, EXPIRATION, + ISSUE DATE:

TSA PRECHECK OR GLOBAL ENTRY NUMBER:

AIRLINE MEMBERSHIP NUMBER:

NOTES (HEALTH/MEDICAL ALERT/PREFERENCES)

passenger
information

PASSENGER 3 (FULL NAME AS SPELLED ON PASSPORT OR ID)

PASSPORT NUMBER, EXPIRATION, + ISSUE DATE:

TSA PRECHECK OR GLOBAL ENTRY NUMBER:

AIRLINE MEMBERSHIP NUMBER:

NOTES (HEALTH/MEDICAL ALERT/PREFERENCES)

PASSENGER 4 (FULL NAME AS SPELLED ON PASSPORT OR ID)

PASSPORT NUMBER, EXPIRATION, + ISSUE DATE:

TSA PRECHECK OR GLOBAL ENTRY NUMBER:

AIRLINE MEMBERSHIP NUMBER:

NOTES (HEALTH/MEDICAL ALERT/PREFERENCES)

PASSENGER 5 (FULL NAME AS SPELLED ON PASSPORT OR ID)

PASSPORT NUMBER, EXPIRATION, + ISSUE DATE:

TSA PRECHECK OR GLOBAL ENTRY NUMBER:

AIRLINE MEMBERSHIP NUMBER:

NOTES (HEALTH/MEDICAL ALERT/PREFERENCES)

passenger information

PASSENGER 6 (FULL NAME AS SPELLED ON PASSPORT OR ID)

PASSPORT NUMBER, EXPIRATION, + ISSUE DATE:

TSA PRECHECK OR GLOBAL ENTRY NUMBER:

AIRLINE MEMBERSHIP NUMBER:

NOTES (HEALTH/MEDICAL ALERT/PREFERENCES)

PASSENGER 7 (FULL NAME AS SPELLED ON PASSPORT OR ID)

PASSPORT NUMBER, EXPIRATION, + ISSUE DATE:

TSA PRECHECK OR GLOBAL ENTRY NUMBER:

AIRLINE MEMBERSHIP NUMBER:

NOTES (HEALTH/MEDICAL ALERT/PREFERENCES)

PASSENGER 8 (FULL NAME AS SPELLED ON PASSPORT OR ID)

PASSPORT NUMBER, EXPIRATION, + ISSUE DATE:

TSA PRECHECK OR GLOBAL ENTRY NUMBER:

AIRLINE MEMBERSHIP NUMBER:

NOTES (HEALTH/MEDICAL ALERT/PREFERENCES)

Vacation Planning

trip research

WHAT I WANT TO FEEL, EXPERIENCE, SEE (WHAT STYLE OF VACATION DO I WANT):

potential destinations

WHERE CAN WE GO? AND BY WHAT ROUTE (FLY, DRIVE, CRUISE, TRAIN, ETC)

BEST DATES TO GO:

potential lodging

WHAT ARE OUR OPTIONS?

activities

WHAT ARE THE TOP ACTIVITIES WE'D LIKE TO EXPERIENCE?

restaurants/pubs

WHAT RESTAURANTS WOULD YOU LIKE TO GO TO?

other elements

IS THERE ANYTHING ELSE YOU'D LIKE TO SEE, DO, OR EXPLORE?

MY NOTES

MY NOTES

MY NOTES

travel budget

DESTINATION: **DURATION OF STAY:**

	ESTIMATED:	ACTUAL:
AIRFARE		
LODGING		
TRANSPORTATION *TO/FROM AIRPORT; TO/FROM LODGING; TO/FROM ACTIVITIES; RETURNING HOME*		
GASOLINE/PETROL		
FOOD *INCLUDE RESTAURANTS, COFFEE/SNACKS; BAR; GROCERIES*		
ACTIVITIES *SHOWS, THEME PARKS/ZOOS, MUSEUMS, PARKS, ADVENTURE, SIGHTSEEING, ETC.*		
PERSONAL CARE *SPAS, POOL, CLASSES, GYM*		
SHOPPING/SOUVENIRS		
CASH *TAXIS, FOOD STANDS, TIPS, SMALL ITEMS, OR IF CREDIT CARDS ARE NOT READILY ACCEPTED EVERYWHERE.*		
OTHER		

FOR TIPS ON HOW TO SAVE MORE MONEY, VISIT
WWW.CRAFTEDTRAVELCO.COM

travel budget

OTHER ITEMS/WORKSPACE

	ESTIMATED:	ACTUAL:

to do list

TO DO:

3/20 — *reserve the activities* ☑

to do list

DATE   TO DO:

_____   _____   ☑

_____   _____   ☐

_____   _____   ☐

_____   _____   ☐

_____   _____   ☐

_____   _____   ☐

_____   _____   ☐

_____   _____   ☐

_____   _____   ☐

_____   _____   ☐

_____   _____   ☐

_____   _____   ☐

_____   _____   ☐

_____   _____   ☐

MY NOTES

MY NOTES

MY NOTES

MY NOTES

MY NOTES

Itinerary Design

travel details

DESTINATION:	DURATION OF STAY:	

FLIGHT DEPARTURE + CONFIRMATION NUMBERS:

FLIGHT DEPARTURE + CONFIRMATION NUMBERS:

LODGING	CONTACT INFORMATION	CONFIRMATION NUMBER
	NOTES	
LODGING	CONTACT INFORMATION	CONFIRMATION NUMBER
	NOTES	
TRANSPORTATION	CONTACT INFORMATION	CONFIRMATION NUMBER
	NOTES	
TRANSPORTATION	CONTACT INFORMATION	CONFIRMATION NUMBER
	NOTES	

travel itinerary

DAY	WHAT TO DO:	CONFIRMATION INFO & NOTES
DAY	WHAT TO DO:	CONFIRMATION INFO & NOTES
DAY	WHAT TO DO:	CONFIRMATION INFO & NOTES
DAY	WHAT TO DO:	CONFIRMATION INFO & NOTES
DAY	WHAT TO DO:	CONFIRMATION INFO & NOTES

NOTES:

travel itinerary

DAY	WHAT TO DO:	CONFIRMATION INFO & NOTES
DAY	WHAT TO DO:	CONFIRMATION INFO & NOTES
DAY	WHAT TO DO:	CONFIRMATION INFO & NOTES
DAY	WHAT TO DO:	CONFIRMATION INFO & NOTES
DAY	WHAT TO DO:	CONFIRMATION INFO & NOTES

NOTES:

....

....

....

travel itinerary

DAY	WHAT TO DO:	CONFIRMATION INFO & NOTES
DAY	WHAT TO DO:	CONFIRMATION INFO & NOTES
DAY	WHAT TO DO:	CONFIRMATION INFO & NOTES
DAY	WHAT TO DO:	CONFIRMATION INFO & NOTES
DAY	WHAT TO DO:	CONFIRMATION INFO & NOTES

NOTES:
....
....
....

travel itinerary

DAY	WHAT TO DO:	CONFIRMATION INFO & NOTES
DAY	WHAT TO DO:	CONFIRMATION INFO & NOTES
DAY	WHAT TO DO:	CONFIRMATION INFO & NOTES
DAY	WHAT TO DO:	CONFIRMATION INFO & NOTES
DAY	WHAT TO DO:	CONFIRMATION INFO & NOTES

NOTES:

logistics checklist

- Transportation to/from airport
- Transportation to/from lodging
- research & obtain passport/visa
- research safety issues & prepare
- What type of payment is generally accepted?
- Where is best to exchange currency?
- What type of transportation options are there?
- Call concierge for recommendations
- Buy travel insurance
- Print copies of all documents
- Leave copy of credit cards/passports with trusted person.
- Check planned activities/sightseeing will be open? (siestas, national holidays, construction...)
- Check for COVID restrictions/requirements
- Time zone concerns (jet lag or will you be up super early at the beginning)
- No more than 1-2 scheduled activities per day
- Call to verify reservations are secured and everyone is expecting your arrival
- Apply for TSA Precheck or Global Entry and make sure the airline has this information
- What will the wifi situation be?
- Will you need a foreign data plan for your phone?
- Download or print directions to all locations (in case you cannot get phone service)
- Download or print transportation schedules if needed (subways, shuttles, etc)
- Will you need a rental car or can you get around via walking, uber, subway, etc?
- Any helpful phrases or words to learn (if traveling to foreign country)?
- Is the water safe to drink?

to do list

DATE   TO DO:

_____   _____ ✓

_____   _____ ☐

_____   _____ ☐

_____   _____ ☐

_____   _____ ☐

_____   _____ ☐

_____   _____ ☐

_____   _____ ☐

_____   _____ ☐

_____   _____ ☐

_____   _____ ☐

_____   _____ ☐

_____   _____ ☐

_____   _____ ☐

_____   _____ ☐

LOGISTICS NOTES

LOGISTICS NOTES

packing list

CLOTHING

TOILETRIES

TECHNOLOGY

SAFETY

NOTES

packing list

WEATHER PROTECTION

BOOKS/ENTERTAINMENT

OFFICIAL DOCUMENTS

MONEY OPTIONS

NOTES

Resources

important numbers

Emergency Numbers by Country/Continent:

Australia	000 (112 on cell phone)
Canada	911
Europe	112
Indonesia	118 (Ambulance), 110 (Police)
Japan	119
Mexico	065 (Ambulance), 060 (Police)
New Zealand	111
Singapore	995
United Kingdom	112 999
USA	911

For more countries, visit
https://travel.state.gov/content/dam/students-abroad/pdfs/911_ABROAD.pdf

Embassies by Citizenship:
Australian Embassies:
https://www.dfat.gov.au/about-us/our-locations/missions/our-embassies-and-consulates-overseas
Canadian Embassies:
https://travel.gc.ca/assistance/embassies-consulates
UK Embassies:
https://www.gov.uk/world/embassies
US Embassies:
https://www.usembassy.gov

language phrases
customize to your location

Hello   Bonjour   (bahn-joor)

currency information
customize to your location

Best places to exchange currency:

Cash will be needed for:

tips

train/subway passes

food carts

How much cash will we need on hand:

Additional notes/reminders:

safety + health information
customize to your location

What has my research said to avoid:

What is the water situation?

Additional notes/reminders:

Metric Conversion Chart

Into Metric

If you know	Multiply by	To Get
Length		
inches	2.54	centimeters
foot	30	centimeters
yards	0.91	meters
miles	1.6	kilometers
Area		
sq. inches	6.5	sq. centimeters
sq. feet	0.09	sq. meters
sq. yards	0.8	sq. meters
sq. miles	2.6	sq. kilometers
Mass (Weight)		
ounces	28	grams
pounds	0.45	kilograms
short ton	0.9	metric ton
Volume		
teaspoons	5	milliliters
tablespoons	15	milliliters
fluid ounces	30	milliliters
cups	0.24	liters
pints	0.47	liters
quarts	0.95	liters
gallons	3.8	liters
cubic feet	0.03	cubic meters
cubic yards	0.76	cubic meters
Temperature		
Fahrenheit	Subtract 32, then multiply by 5/9ths to get	Celsius

Out of Metric

If you know	Multiply by	To Get
Length		
millimeters	0.04	inches
centimeters	0.4	inches
meters	3.3	feet
kilometers	0.62	miles
Area		
sq. centimeters	0.16	sq. inches
sq. meters	1.2	sq. yards
sq. kilometers	0.4	sq. miles
hectares	2.47	acres
Mass (Weight)		
grams	0.035	ounces
kilograms	2.2	pounds
metric tons	1.1	short tons
Volume		
milliliters	0.03	fluid ounces
liters	2.1	pints
liters	1.06	quarts
liters	0.26	gallons
cubic meters	35	cubic feet
cubic meters	1.3	cubic yards
Temperature		
Celsius	Multiply by 9/5ths, then add 32 to get	Fahrenheit

Journal

MEMORIES

DATE _____

Today I went:

I met:

I had this happen:

But the most memorable thing was:

MEMORIES

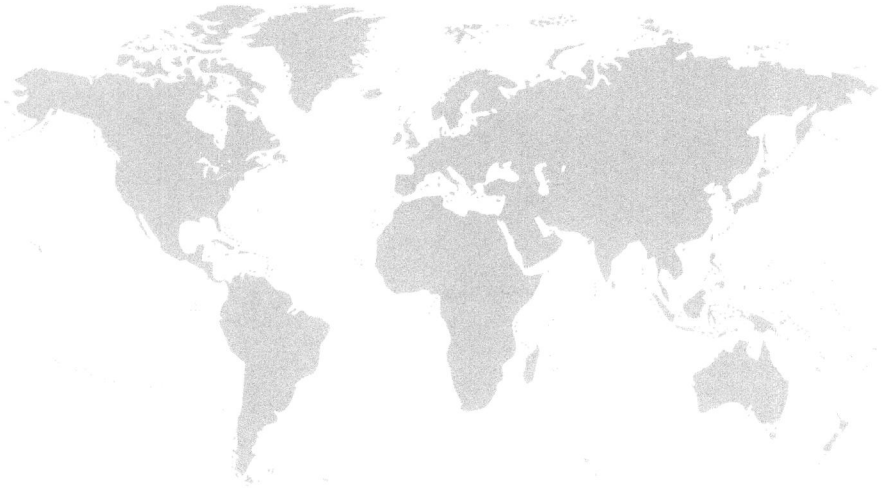

DATE _____

Today I went:

_____

_____

I met:

_____

_____

I had this happen:

_____

_____

_____

_____

But the most memorable thing was:

_____

_____

_____

_____

_____

_____

_____

_____

_____

_____

MEMORIES

DATE _____

Today I went:

_____

_____

I met:

_____

_____

I had this happen:

_____

_____

_____

_____

But the most memorable thing was:

_____

_____

_____

_____

_____

_____

_____

_____

_____

_____

MEMORIES

DATE _____

Today I went:

I met:

I had this happen:

But the most memorable thing was:

MEMORIES

DATE _____

Today I went:

I met:

I had this happen:

But the most memorable thing was:

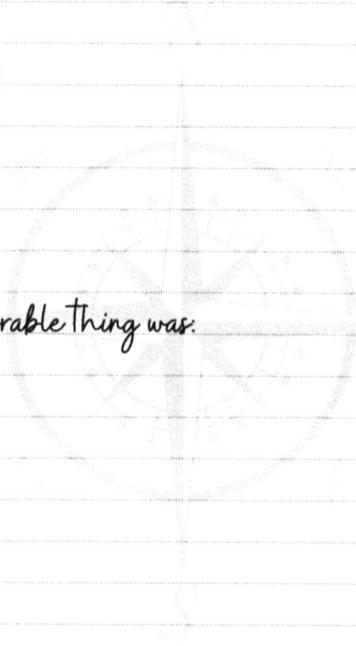

MEMORIES

DATE _____

Today I went:

I met:

I had this happen:

But the most memorable thing was:

MEMORIES

DATE _____

Today I went:

_____

_____

I met:

_____

_____

I had this happen:

_____

_____

_____

But the most memorable thing was:

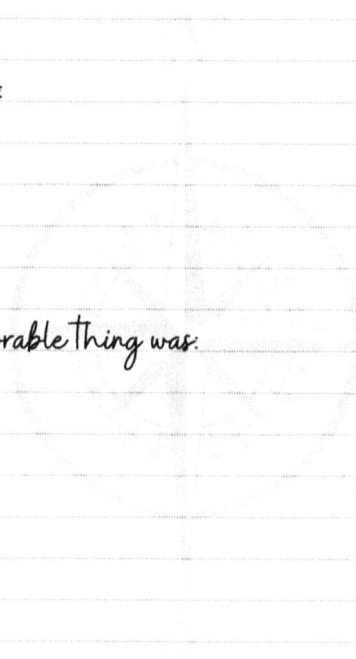

_____

_____

_____

_____

_____

_____

_____

_____

_____

_____

_____

MEMORIES

DATE _____

Today I went:
_____
_____

I met:
_____
_____

I had this happen:
_____
_____
_____
_____

But the most memorable thing was:
_____
_____
_____
_____
_____
_____
_____
_____
_____
_____
_____

MEMORIES

DATE _____

Today I went:

I met:

I had this happen:

But the most memorable thing was:

MEMORIES

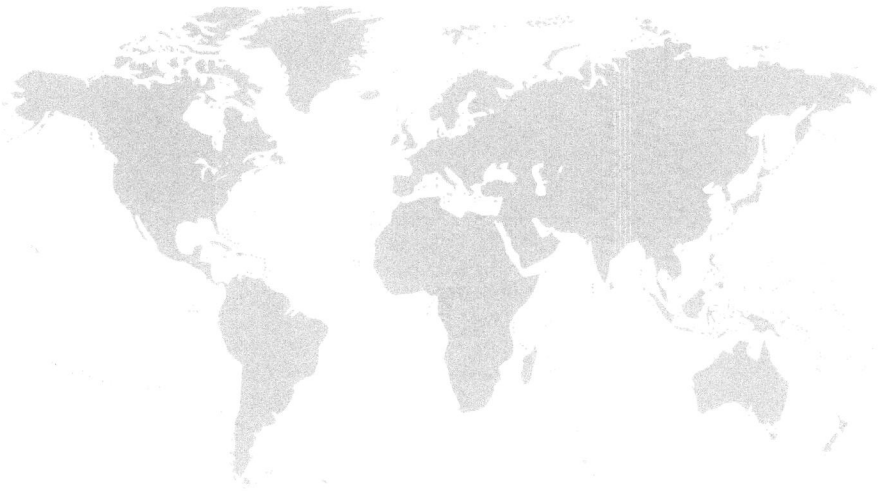

DATE _____

Today I went:

I met:

I had this happen:

But the most memorable thing was:

MEMORIES

DATE _____

Today I went:

I met:

I had this happen:

But the most memorable thing was:

MEMORIES

DATE _____

Today I went:

I met:

I had this happen:

But the most memorable thing was:

MEMORIES

DATE _____

Today I went:

I met:

I had this happen:

But the most memorable thing was:

MEMORIES

DATE _____

Today I went:

I met:

I had this happen:

But the most memorable thing was:

MEMORIES

DATE _____

Today I went:

I met:

I had this happen:

But the most memorable thing was:

MEMORIES

DATE _____

Today I went:

I met:

I had this happen:

But the most memorable thing was:

MEMORIES

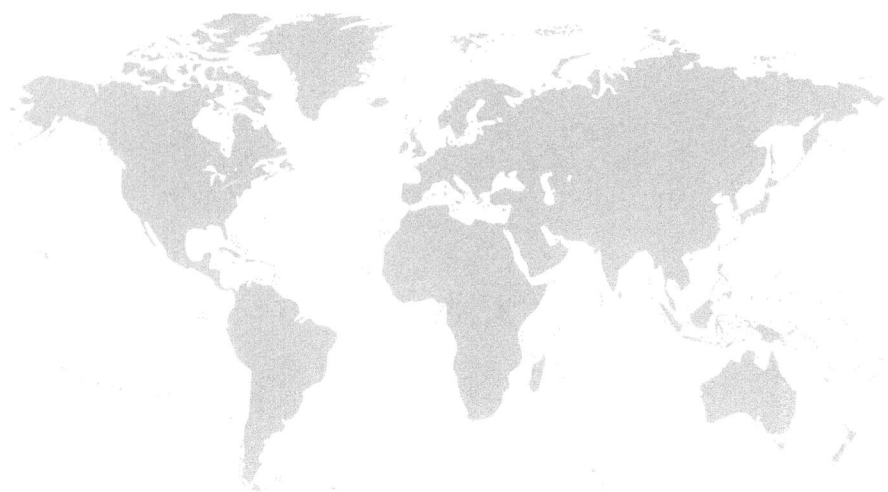

DATE _____

Today I went:

_____

_____

I met:

_____

_____

I had this happen:

_____

_____

_____

But the most memorable thing was:

_____

_____

_____

_____

_____

_____

_____

_____

_____

_____

MEMORIES

DATE _____

Today I went:
....
....

I met:
....
....

I had this happen:
....
....
....
....

But the most memorable thing was:
....
....
....
....
....
....
....
....
....
....
....

MEMORIES

DATE _____

Today I went:

_____

_____

I met:

_____

_____

I had this happen:

_____

_____

_____

But the most memorable thing was:

_____

_____

_____

_____

_____

_____

_____

_____

_____

_____

_____

MEMORIES

DATE _____

Today I went:

_____

_____

I met:

_____

_____

I had this happen:

_____

_____

_____

But the most memorable thing was:

_____

_____

_____

_____

_____

_____

_____

_____

_____

MEMORIES

DATE _____

Today I went:

I met:

I had this happen:

But the most memorable thing was:

MEMORIES

DATE _____

Today I went:

_____

_____

I met:

_____

_____

I had this happen:

_____

_____

_____

But the most memorable thing was:

_____

_____

_____

_____

_____

_____

_____

_____

_____

MEMORIES

DATE _____

Today I went:

_____
_____

I met:

_____
_____

I had this happen:

_____
_____
_____
_____

But the most memorable thing was:

_____
_____
_____
_____
_____
_____
_____
_____
_____

MEMORIES

DATE _____

Today I went:
_____
_____

I met:
_____
_____

I had this happen:
_____
_____
_____

But the most memorable thing was:
_____
_____
_____
_____
_____
_____
_____
_____
_____

MEMORIES

DATE _____

Today I went:

_____

_____

I met:

_____

_____

I had this happen:

_____

_____

_____

_____

But the most memorable thing was:

_____

_____

_____

_____

_____

_____

_____

_____

_____

_____

MEMORIES

DATE _____

Today I went:

_____

_____

I met:

_____

_____

I had this happen:

_____

_____

_____

_____

But the most memorable thing was:

_____

_____

_____

_____

_____

_____

_____

_____

_____

MEMORIES

DATE _____

Today I went:

I met:

I had this happen:

But the most memorable thing was:

MEMORIES

DATE _____

Today I went:

_____

_____

I met:

_____

_____

I had this happen:

_____

_____

_____

But the most memorable thing was:

_____

_____

_____

_____

_____

_____

_____

_____

_____

MEMORIES

D A T E _____

Today I went:

_____
_____

I met:

_____
_____

I had this happen:

_____
_____
_____

But the most memorable thing was:

_____
_____
_____
_____
_____
_____
_____
_____
_____

MEMORIES

DATE _____

Today I went:

_____
_____

I met:

_____
_____

I had this happen:

_____
_____
_____

But the most memorable thing was:

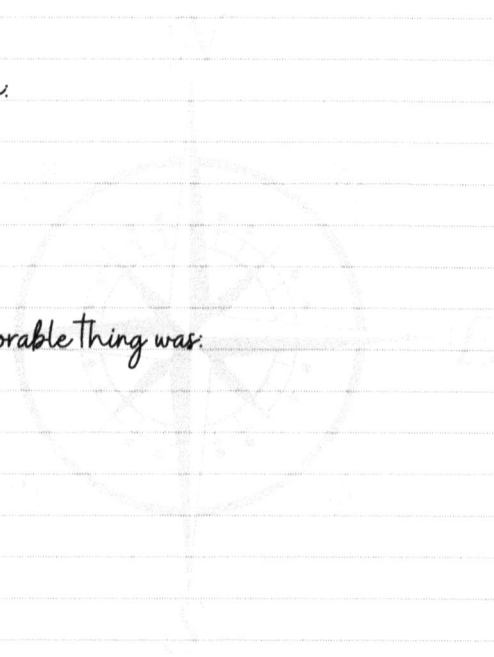

_____
_____
_____
_____
_____
_____
_____
_____
_____

Made in the USA
Monee, IL
09 July 2021